IMAGES
of Sports

FOOTBALL AT
BALL STATE UNIVERSITY
1924–2001

From 1924 to 1967, Ball State played its home football games at Ball Recreation Field, sometimes called Ball Athletic Field. The football field was located on University Avenue across from Ball Memorial Hospital. Seating capacity was listed at 9,000 but in the 1950s and 1960s crowds frequently surpassed 10,000 as the overflow spectators took places on the grass along the sidelines and in the end zones.

IMAGES
of Sports

FOOTBALL AT
BALL STATE UNIVERSITY
1924–2001

E. Bruce Geelhoed

ARCADIA

Published by Arcadia Publishing,
an imprint of Tempus Publishing, Inc.
3047 N. Lincoln Ave., Suite 410
Chicago, IL 60657

Printed in Great Britain.

Library of Congress Catalog Card Number: 2001091279

For all general information contact Arcadia Publishing at:
Telephone 843-853-2070
Fax 843-853-0044
E-Mail sales@arcadiapublishing.com

For customer service and orders:
Toll-Free 1-888-313-2665

Visit us on the internet at http://www.arcadiapublishing.com

Former coach Ray Louthen and several of his players gathered for this photograph at one of the alumni golf outings. Included in the photo, from left to right, are Chuck Streetman, George Hathaway, Mike Furimsky, Ted Huber, Coach Ray Louthen, George McKay, Norm Troth, Steve Midkiff, Terry Bonta, and John Shipley.

CONTENTS

ACKNOWLEDGEMENTS

I wish to thank a number of helpful people who have assisted me with the completion of this book about the history of the football program at Ball State University. First, the staff of the Athletic Communications office at Ball State was indispensable. Joseph D. Hernandez, director of Athletics Communications, made the photo files of his office available and I discovered a treasure of photography relating to intercollegiate football. Robin Brown, secretary to Joseph Hernandez, was likewise indispensable. Without her assistance, and that of the numerous student assistants who pulled photo files for me, this book could not have been written. Thanks to the office of Photographic Sevices for their excellent photographic collection on Ball State athletics. I am also grateful to Muncie Newspapers, Inc. for permission to use several of its photos in Chapter 4 of the book.

Second, I want to acknowledge the work of Jerry Cole, education media coordinator in the Video Information System at Ball State. Jerry helped me with my previous *Images of America* book, *Muncie: The Middletown of America*, and he handled most of the production work relating to the photographs used in the book. Julie Gibboney, student assistant in the Center for Middletown Studies, also spent countless hours chasing down photographs which became part of the book. John Straw, director of archives and special collections at Ball State, also helped on this project as he had on my previous book. SangMi Cho, student assistant in Ball State's archives and special collections, was also helpful.

Third, I wish to thank Edwin Shipley, director of Alumni Affairs at Ball State, and Bill Lynch, Ball State's head football coach, for their assistance. Ed was able to provide some useful information about the post-graduation careers of many Cardinal footballers, and Bill shared some insights about the contributions of many football players, insights which have not been generally reported.

Finally, this book is dedicated to Ball State's football players and coaches, past and present. Many of the players included in this book have also been inducted into the Ball State University Athletic Hall of Fame. They are denoted in the text by the abbreviation (BSUAHF-year.) The football program belongs to all of its players, coaches, and supporters, however, and one of the inescapable limitations in a book of this type is that the author must be selective about its content. I trust that this book will not only recognize some of the key people and highlights from the Ball State football tradition, but also bring back some poignant moments from a story which is central to Ball State's history as an institution of higher education. Any errors of fact and interpretation are mine.

E. Bruce Geelhoed

INTRODUCTION

On October 18, 1924, the Hoosieroons of Ball Teachers College in Muncie, Indiana traveled to Terre Haute, Indiana to play a football game against the Sycamores of the Indiana State Normal School. It was the first football game in the history of Ball Teachers College, later Ball State Teachers College (1929–1965), and then Ball State University (1965–present). The Sycamores won the contest, 47-0, an outcome not surprising since the school from Muncie had never fielded a football team before 1924. But the game between the two schools was unique: in reality, it was almost an intramural-type contest since Ball Teachers College was the eastern division, or the branch campus, of Indiana State. Nevertheless, the game provided a glimpse into the future: by putting a football team on the field, Ball Teachers College was preparing for the time when it would become an independent institution with its own comprehensive academic and athletic programs. In February 1929 the Indiana General Assembly passed legislation which enabled Ball Teachers College to become a separate institution. Ball State Teachers College had become Indiana's fourth publicly assisted institution of higher education, joining Indiana University, Purdue University, and Indiana State Teachers College. Although Ball State had become a separate institution from Indiana State, the two schools maintained their rivalry in football throughout much of the 20th century.

During the 1920s, the football team at Ball Teachers College helped the school in its effort to create a separate identity from Indiana State. On November 7, 1924, Ball Teachers College won its first football game when it defeated Central Normal (from Danville, Indiana) at home, 9-6. Three years later, football had gained respectability at the college as the Hoosieroons, re-named the Cardinals in 1927, put together three successive winning seasons in 1926, 1927, and 1928. Once the school obtained independent status in 1929, the athletic program, and the football program in particular, helped the school carve out its niche in Midwestern higher education.

As Ball State Teachers College, the football program competed in two separate eras. First, between 1924–1950, Ball State was a member of the Indiana Intercollegiate Conference (IIC) and competed in football primarily against other small colleges in Indiana. Over this period, the Cardinals developed spirited rivalries with such schools as Hanover College, Wabash College, Earlham College, DePauw University, Valparaiso University, and especially Butler University and Indiana State Teachers College. Second, between 1950 and 1968 the Cardinals competed in the Indiana Collegiate Conference (ICC), maintaining their rivalries with the Indiana schools but also adding institutions of similar size and purpose in neighboring states, including Miami University of Ohio, Eastern Michigan University, Southern Illinois University, Illinois State University, and Northern Illinois University, to the schedule.

By the beginning of the 1970s, Ball State had a student enrollment which exceeded 15,000 students, and its football program had clearly surpassed the day when its schedule could primarily consist of the state's liberal arts colleges. In 1973, Ball State gained admission to the

Mid-American Conference (MAC), joining Eastern Michigan, Central Michigan, Western Michigan, Northern Illinois, Miami University, the University of Toledo, Ohio University, Bowling Green, and Kent State. Entry to the MAC confirmed NCAA Division I status for Ball State's football program, and its players and coaches rose to the occasion by winning two conference championships, 1976 and 1978, in the school's first five years as a participant in football. In 1976, moreover, Ball State became the first non-Ohio school to win an outright championship in football.

Since joining the MAC, Ball State has consistently fielded competitive football teams while strengthening its schedule to include instate rivals Indiana University and Purdue University, other Big Ten schools such as the University of Wisconsin and the University of Minnesota, as well as such other major football powers as the University of Florida, the University of Kansas, and Auburn University. Thus, the football profile at Ball State in 2001 is considerably different from 1924. Over the course of the past 75 years, Ball State's football program has produced numerous conference champions; several Cardinal footballers have earned All-American and Academic All-American awards; many players have gone on to successful, productive careers in the professional ranks, either in American football leagues or abroad; and a large contingent of Cardinal players have pursued coaching careers at the high school, collegiate, and professional levels. This book proposes to tell the story of Ball State football: its players, its coaches, its traditions, and the larger football scene.

Fans turn out for college football on a Saturday in Muncie. A full house at Ball State Stadium watches the Cardinals in action. Spectators have always enjoyed a tradition of observing the game from the grassy banks along the fences.

AUTUMN IN MUNCIE
The Return of Ball State Football

Autumn in the Midwest means a new school year—and a new football season. For people in central Indiana, the college team to follow has been the Ball State Cardinals. Football games create memories: of exciting plays on the field, of cheering crowds, of an enthusiastic musical program put on by the Ball State Marching Band, and the experience of sunny afternoons in September and October, as well as cold and rainy ones in November.

With the Ball State Marching Band, "The Pride of Mid-America," playing in the background, Ball State's football team charges onto the field.

This drawing is an artist's conception of Ball State Stadium, home of the Cardinals since the middle of the 1967 season.

An enthusiastic group of Ball State students cheers on the Cardinals.

THE HOMECOMING TRADITION

PUT THE ACES IN ORBIT

Football is synonymous with the observance of homecoming on college and university campuses. Ball State's homecomings have traditionally featured a parade with floats constructed by student organizations. This float was entered when Ball State played the University of Evansville in its traditional homecoming game.

The Ball State Marching Band performed a complicated program during halftime of the Homecoming game in 1937.

In 1959, John R. Emens, Ball State's president, congratulated the homecoming queen, Nicki Negangard, and the members of her court. Emens served as Ball State's president from 1945 to 1968, and was an enthusiastic supporter of the athletic program. During his presidency, the school significantly expanded its athletic facilities, adding not only Ball State Stadium for the football team, but also University Gym (now Irving Gym), University Pool (now the Lewellen Aquatic Center), additional tennis courts, and new baseball and soccer fields. Emens was inducted, posthumously, into the Ball State University Athletic Hall of Fame in 1977.

Members of a Ball State fraternity attend homecoming festivities in 1965 dressed in their fur coats.

The Ball State homecoming game in 1996 attracted a large crowd. In 1996, Ball State continued an expansion of its seating capacity in the stadium from 16,300 to more than 18,000 spectators. The current seating capacity of the stadium is 21,600.

COACHING THE CARDINALS

Ball State's football program has been guided over the years by 12 head coaches: Paul B. (Billy) Williams, Norman Wann, Paul Parker, Lawrence McPhee, John Magnabosco, George Serdula, Jim Freeman, Wave Myers, Dave McClain, Dwight Wallace, Paul Schudel, and Bill Lynch. Each of the coaches directed the team during a specific era and each left his mark on the progress of the program.

Billy Williams was the head football coach in 1924, 1925, and 1929. Williams is considered the father of Ball State athletics. At one time during the 1920s, Williams coached all of the major sports: football, baseball, basketball, and track and field. He was also the school's first athletic director and head of its department of physical education. Williams was inducted into the Ball State University Athletic Hall of Fame, posthumously, in 1976. His football teams compiled a record of 3–13.

John Magnabosco was the head football coach from 1935 to 1952. Magnabosco was Ball State's first football coach of the modern era. His teams compiled an overall record of 68–46–14. He was inducted, posthumously, into the Ball State University Athletic Hall of Fame in 1976.

In this photo, Magnabosco is shown with two assistant coaches, George Serdula, left, and Richard Stealy, right. In 1953, Serdula succeeded Magnabosco as the head football coach and held the post until 1955. His teams compiled an overall record of 14–9–1. Stealy was a former football player under Magnabosco who returned to his alma mater as a coach and member of the department of physical education.

15

Jim Freeman was the head football coach from 1956 to 1961. Freeman coached the Cardinals for six seasons and his teams compiled an overall record of 18–28–2. Freeman's best season occurred in 1959, when his team went 6–2 and were conference co-champions.

Ray Louthen was the head football coach from 1962 to 1967. Under Louthen's direction, the Cardinals went 37–13–3. Louthen also coached the baseball team during the 1960s and was Ball State's athletic director between 1970 and 1981. In the period from 1960 to 1980, Louthen was clearly the leader of Ball State's athletic program. He was inducted into the Ball State Athletic Hall of Fame in 1976.

Wave Myers was the head football coach from 1968 to 1970. Formerly an assistant coach under Ray Louthen, Wave Myers coached the Cardinal football team during its first three full years in the new Ball State Stadium. Under Myers's leadership, the Cardinals posted a 15–14 record. Myers was a Ball State alumnus who was a successful high school football coach before returning to his alma mater's football program. He was chosen as high school Coach of the Year by the Ball State University Alumni Association in 1958, and was inducted into the Ball State University Athletic Hall of Fame in 1989.

Dave McClain was the head football coach from 1971 to 1977. Under McClain's leadership, Ball State entered competition in the Mid-American Conference in 1975. During his tenure, the Cardinals compiled a 46–25–3 record, winning their first conference championship in 1976. Popular and energetic, McClain developed a program that moved the Cardinals to the front ranks of football competition. In 1977, McClain left Ball State to become the head football coach at the University of Wisconsin. In 1986, he died tragically from a heart attack, and the Big Ten Conference has named its football coach of the year award in his honor. McClain was inducted into the Ball State University Athletic Hall of Fame, posthumously, in 1990.

Dwight Wallace was the head football coach from 1978 to 1984. Ball State's football teams went 40–37 during Wallace's tenure, including a 10–1 record and a MAC championship in 1978. Wallace succeeded Ray Louthen as Ball State's athletic director in 1981, and served briefly in that post.

Paul Schudel was the head football coach from 1985 to 1994. During Schudel's tenure, the Cardinals compiled a 55–43–3 record, winning MAC championships in 1989 and 1993. Schudel also took the Cardinals to the California Raisin Bowl in 1989, their first bowl appearance in 22 years. Schudel's championship team in 1993 played in the Las Vegas Bowl.

Bill Lynch has been the head football coach from 1995 to the present. Lynch was an assistant football coach at Ball State between 1990 and 1992. He left and accepted a position as the quarterback's coach at Indiana University. He returned to Ball State as head football coach in 1995. Under his leadership, in 1996, the Cardinals won their fourth MAC championship.

A WINNING TRADITION

Through the efforts of the athletic department and the Ball State University Alumni Association, the University recognizes its successful coaches and players at various events scheduled throughout the year. Given the strong bond which exists between former players, and former players and their coaches, these gatherings take on an added significance with each year that passes.

Ball State's 1949 team, coached by John Magnabosco, went undefeated in its eight games. Members of the team gathered for their 50th anniversary reunion on October 30, 1999.

Top: Ball State's 1978 team, Mid-American champions coached by Dwight Wallace, gathered for this photograph at their 20th reunion in 1978.

Bottom left: Bill Reynolds, a baseball player at Ball State in the 1930s, was the team's longtime volunteer assistant coach who worked with the punters and placekickers. Reynolds is seen in this picture with player Mike Harrison prior to a game against Indiana State in the Hoosier Dome (later the RCA Dome) in Indianapolis. Reynolds was inducted into the Ball State University Athletic Hall of Fame in 1996.

Bottom right: Earl Yestingsmeier, a Ball State alumnus and the school's longtime golf coach, was sports information director between 1959 and 1980. Most of the photographs used in this book were drawn from the files which Yestingsmeier maintained during his tenure as Ball State's athletic spokesman. He was inducted into the Ball State University Athletic Hall of Fame in 1981.

One

THE EARLY YEARS
1924–1935

During its first decade, Ball State's football program underwent a series of changes. First, the team experienced numerous changes in the head coaching position. Paul (Billy) Williams coached the team during its first two years, 1924 and 1925, before turning the responsibility over to Norman "Happy" Wann, who was the head coach in 1926 and 1927. Wann was succeeded by Paul "Shorty" Parker in 1928, and Billy Williams returned to coach the team in 1929. In 1930, Ball State hired Lawrence McPhee as head football coach and he coached the team for the next five seasons.

Second, any type of intercollegiate athletics was a new enterprise at Ball State. Between 1924 and 1929, the school was the branch campus of Indiana State but competed in the Indiana Intercollegiate Conference, along with Indiana State, as an independent member. Between 1924 and 1927, the school's teams were known as the Hoosieroons, clearly borrowing from the tradition of the Indiana Hoosiers. Dissatisfaction with that name quickly emerged, however, and in 1927, the school changed its mascot to the Cardinals, after a campus-wide contest to choose a new symbol. Billy Williams nominated the name Cardinals because his favorite baseball team was the St. Louis Cardinals.

Third, Ball State lacked an athletic tradition, and building such a tradition was part of the task confronting the school's coaches and players during the formative years of its athletic program. Not that enthusiasm for football was lacking, but clearly the school was without a nucleus of skilled players. "Forty-five men responded to the call [for football players] issued by Coach Williams last fall," wrote a reporter for *The Orient*, the campus yearbook, in 1925. "Only five of these men had any previous football experience." Likewise, as a teacher-training institution, Ball State was not necessarily the first choice of outstanding high school athletes who were looking for the best college to continue their athletic careers. "Williams's great problem is that of transforming school teachers into athletes," one campus observer wrote in the 1920s.

Despite the obvious handicaps, the football program developed a following and a claim on the imagination of the Ball State campus in its first decade. By the mid-1930s, Ball State had a football tradition which served as its foundation for the future.

To the left is Paul (Billy) Williams as he appeared early in his career at Ball State. The coach of multiple sports and the school's head physical educator, Williams laid the foundation for Ball State's athletic program. "He is a friend to every athlete in the school, and everyone on the campus has a big, broad smile for our coach," wrote a reporter for *The Orient*.

Williams was a member of the Ball State faculty and athletic administration from 1921 until his retirement in 1958. As a coach, he was primarily known for his leadership of the baseball team which he coached continuously throughout his career at Ball State.

Top left: Lawrence McPhee coached football at Ball State between 1930 and 1934. McPhee's first team, the 1930 squad, posted a 6–1 record, but his next four teams were only mediocre.
Top right: Norman "Happy" Wann was the head football coach at Ball Teachers College in 1926 and 1927. Despite his brief tenure, Wann had two fine seasons and his career record was 10–3–2.
Bottom right: Virgil "Pop" Schooler was a four-sport athlete at Ball Teacher Colleges in the 1920s, excelling in football, baseball, basketball, and track. He scored the winning touchdown in the college's victory over Manchester College in 1927. (BSUAHF-1978).

Frank Chase captained Ball Teachers College's first football team in 1924. He sustained a broken neck during a game against Oakland City College in 1926. Chase recovered from his injuries and returned to school in 1927. He was the student manager of the football team in 1928. (BSUAHF-1978)

Ball Teachers College's 1926 football squad competed when the school was still a branch campus of the Indiana State Normal School at Terre Haute. The "N" monogram on the player's uniform presumably refers to the word "Normal."

By 1930, Ball State had received separate collegiate status. Its 1930 team was considerably better equipped than the 1926 squad.

An unidentified Ball Teachers College gridder strains for the goal line during a game in 1926. The team's opponent that day apparently lacked sufficient funds to provide helmets for all of its players.

By 1930, football had become a popular sport on campus. This picture, included in *The Orient*, shows three Cardinal players set against the backdrop of a pigskin.

One of Ball State's spirited rivals during its first decade was Earlham College, located nearby in Richmond, Indiana. This photo reveals the close-in contact characteristic of football during that period. Ball State players are wearing the dark helmets; Earlham players are wearing white helmets.

In 1926, Coach Norman Wann took his football team to Camp Crosley in northern Indiana for two weeks of practice before beginning the regular season. Camp Crosley was operated by the Muncie YMCA, and partially funded by donations from members of the Ball family. The camp was named in memory of Crosley Ball, a son of Edmund B. Ball and his wife Bertha Crosley Ball. The youngster had died following complications from a tonsillectomy.

Ball Teachers College players line up for drills at Camp Crosley. Note the corn field in the background.

Top: Regular scrimmages were part of the routine at Camp Crosley.

Middle: Gridders attack the blocking sleds while at Camp Crosley. As a reporter for *The Orient* wrote, "In order to get his team in condition for the strenuous football schedule arranged for them, Coach Norman G. Wann took his football warriors to school two weeks before school opened. From early morning until late at night, the Camp Crosley gridiron resounded with the strenuous efforts of the Cardinal warriors. The squad members ran the boxes, bucked the sled, kicked the pigskin, and scrimmaged daily."

Bottom: In 1929, the Cardinal football team journeyed to Kentucky for a game against Western Kentucky. During the trip, they stopped for a visit to Mammoth Cave, the setting for this team picture. Western Kentucky won the football game, 13-0.

Two

THE MAGNABOSCO ERA
1935–1952

Ball State's football fortunes took a serious turn in the mid-1930s with the hiring of John Magnabosco as the head football coach. Magnabosco had been a successful football player at Indiana University who won three letters in 1927, 1928, and 1929. After receiving his masters degree at Indiana University, he pursued a teaching and coaching career at the high school level. His coaching assignment before arriving at Ball State was at Clinton High School in northwest Indiana where his teams "were the terror of the state," in the words of one Ball State student reporter.

Magnabosco took over a program which had been unsuccessful for the previous four years, and interest in football on campus appeared to be lagging. The football outlook was so poor that "the Cardinals were the pushover, the lollipops, the doormats of the Secondary [IIC] Conference." When Magnabosco began his coaching career at Ball State, there were "not enough prospects reporting for football to crowd Dean [Ralph] Noyer's office." But Magnabosco's disciplined style and attention to detail quickly paid off with winning seasons. After two average seasons in 1935 and 1936, Magnabosco had three outstanding seasons in 1937, 1938, and 1939 where the Cardinals posted a 17–4–1 period over that stretch. Magnabosco's teams continued to post winning records throughout the years of World War II, when the entire athletic program was de-emphasized. These were the years when the football team consisted of true student-athletes who played without the financial benefit of generous athletic grants. "Our boys are not subsidized in any respect," wrote a reporter for *The Orient* in 1939. "They are not the inevitable parasites that the popular mind believes college football players invariably are."

During the late 1940s, the Cardinals returned to their winning ways with three splendid seasons in 1947, 1948, and 1949. The Cardinals posted a 14 game winning streak in 1948–1949. The 1949 team went undefeated through eight games, the first Cardinal football team to accomplish that feat. Magnabosco's teams also won several conference championships and maintained the storied rivalry between Ball State and Butler University, coached by Tony Hinkle, which developed during the 1930s.

Magnabosco's unique name was a constant target for nicknaming, too. Known on campus as Uncle John, the Big Boss, Mag, the Big Mag, or more commonly simply as Maggie, the football coach was one of Ball State's most visible personalities. (Occasionally the football team was also described as the Maggiepies.) A man with a "lusty, earthy air about him that anyone within a gun shot can't resist," Magnabosco had "a tremendous amount of fun with the boys." Magnabosco's success with the football program resulted in larger crowds to watch the team on Saturdays and the development of players who would always be associated with stardom in Cardinal athletics. During the Magnabosco Era, the Cardinals played a number of memorable games, including the 1938 contest against Manchester College where the Cardinals came back from a 14 point deficit to win, 15–14. Magnabosco's impact upon the football program was so enormous that, beginning in 1959, the award given to Ball State's most valuable player has been named the John Magnabosco Award.

In a familiar pose, Coach John Magnabosco prepared for another football practice at Ball Athletic Field.

Better known for his exploits as Ball State's basketball coach and tennis coach, Branch McCracken was also an assistant football coach during the 1930s, mainly coaching the freshman squad. McCracken left Ball State in 1938 to accept the head basketball coaching position at Indiana University where he coached for the next three decades, winning two NCAA championships, in 1940 and 1953, respectively, and several Big Ten championships. He was inducted into the Ball State University Athletic Hall of Fame, posthumously, in 1976.

Magnabosco sported a new uniform style for the 1938 season, one borrowed from the look of the professional football team, the Chicago Cardinals.

Ball State's 1938 team sported striped jerseys, a departure from their conservative uniform of previous seasons.

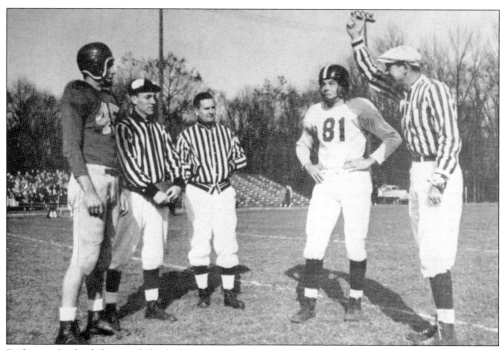

Referees also had their stylish clothing, as demonstrated by the Ivy League cap worn by a referee who is looking over the pre-game flip of the coin.

STANDOUTS FROM THE MAGNABOSCO ERA

During John Magnabosco's coaching career, a number of Cardinal footballers became noted for their football prowess, winning all-conference honors and also strengthening the entire program.

Mel Wilson played football at Ball State from 1933 to 1936. He played the end and tackle positions as well as handled the punting and placekicking duties. Wilson also competed in basketball and track for the Cardinals. (BSUAHF-1978)

Dick Stealy was a three-sport standout for Ball State between 1938 and 1941, competing in football, basketball, and track. He played the center position on offense, and was also a defensive lineman. Following his graduation from Ball State, he returned to his alma mater where he enjoyed a long and successful coaching career. He served as head basketball coach between 1948 and 1952, head track coach between 1954 and 1967, head cross country coach between 1956 and 1966, and assistant football coach between 1946 and 1957. (BSUAHF-1977)

Gabor (Gabe) Takats was a standout lineman for Ball State between 1937 and 1940. An all-conference performer, Takats was referred to by student reporters as a "gladiator who tackled first and asked questions later." Following his graduation, Takats was also a successful high school football coach. (BSUAHF-1985)

Walter Pesavento competed in football for Ball State between 1936 and 1938. An all-conference performer in 1937 and 1938, Pesavento played fullback, linebacker, and punter. He was also an outstanding baseball player who once struck out 17 batters in one game in 1938. (BSUAHF-1982)

Hubert "Hub" Etchison was an end on the Ball State football teams of the late 1930s. Etchison is perhaps better known for his exploits as the very successful football coach of the Richmond (high school) Red Devils. Etchison won Ball State's high school coach of the year award four times, in 1961, 1962, 1963, and 1967. He was instrumental in the establishment of the Indiana Football Coaches Association and the Indiana Football Hall of Fame. (BSUAHF-1976)

Waymond Ferguson was a durable running back for Ball State in the late 1930s.

Dale Miller played quarterback for Ball State in 1936, 1937, and 1938. Like most football players of the era, Miller played on both offense and defense. In 1937 and 1938 he led Ball State to season records of 5–2–1 and 6–1–1. In 1961 Miller accepted a position on Ball State's professional staff where he worked until his retirement in 1981. (BSUAHF-1984)

James (Jimmy) Phend played halfback for the Cardinals between 1938 and 1940. Ball State's first running back with "breakaway speed," Phend was known as the "Goshen Ghost" because of his shifty, elusive running style. In 1938, he led the conference in scoring. Following graduation, Phend served in both World War II and the Korean War where he compiled a distinguished military record. (BSUAHF-1979)

A glimpse at the Ball State bench during the 1940s shows a group of players intently watching the action on the field.

One of Ball State's running backs gains ground in a game played during the early 1940s.

In 1946, Ball State had an overflow crowd for its homecoming game. The expressions on the faces of the students and spectators revealed a new spirit of optimism and confidence on campus after the difficult years of World War II. In 1946, Ball State also recorded its first victory in football over Butler University, coached by Tony Hinkle.

Jim Davidson, an interior lineman who anchored Ball State's offensive line, played for the Cardinals in 1936, 1937, and 1938. He was a member of Coach Magnabosco's first recruiting class. Davidson was an all-conference selection during his junior and senior years. (BSUAHF-1983)

Fred Kehoe was a standout performer for Ball State between 1946 and 1949. Playing halfback, he was the leading scorer on the 1949 team. Kehoe also participated in basketball and track as a collegian and later returned to Ball State as an assistant coach in several sports and as an athletic administrator. (BSUAHF-1976)

This is the team photograph for Ball State's 1949 team, undefeated in eight games and conference champions.

Following their championship season, the members of the 1949 team and their coaches celebrated with a banquet in their honor at the Pine Shelf room on campus.

Three
THE 1950S AND 1960S

John Magnabosco stepped down as Ball State's head football coach in 1952, ending his lengthy tenure as the leader of the Cardinals. George Serdula, Magnabosco's successor, coached the football team for the next three seasons, compiling a 14–9–1 record during that brief period. In 1956, Jim Freeman became Ball State's head football coach. In 1959, the Cardinals posted a 6–2 record and were co-champions of the Indiana Collegiate Conference, but for most of Freeman's tenure, which lasted until 1961, Ball State's football fortunes took a step backward. In 1962, Ray Louthen became Ball State's head football coach, adding the football responsibility to his other main coaching position, head baseball coach. The program picked up immediately under Louthen's leadership, and he led the Cardinals to six successive winning seasons, three conference championships, and two trips to the Grantland Rice Bowl. Not since the late 1940s and the late 1930s had the Cardinals turned in such an impressive performance in football. Louthen stepped down as football coach after the 1967 season, and Wave Myers, one of his assistants, took over the program. A Ball State alumnus, Myers coached the football team until 1970, compiling a 15–14 record. During the tenure of Wave Myers, the Cardinals moved permanently into the new Ball State Stadium north of the main campus.

The 1950s and 1960s were noteworthy for several reasons. First, enthusiasm for the football program grew on campus and in the community. More athletes turned out to participate in the football program and the crowds at the games on University Avenue grew ever larger. Ball State received university status in 1965 when its student enrollment reached 10,000, ending the years when Ball State competed as a teachers college. Both campus and community turned out in ever-growing numbers to watch the Cardinals and the hard-nosed brand of football which they played. The larger crowds were treated to some truly exciting contests. For example, the Cardinals rallied from a 16-point deficit in 1959 to defeat DePauw University, 30-24. They came back from a 15-point deficit to defeat St. Joseph's University, 42-19 and preserve their undefeated record in 1965.

Second, the football program grew in quality as well as quantity. Such Cardinal standouts as running backs Tim Brown and Jim Todd, and lineman Chuck Streetman, signed contracts with professional teams in the National Football League and played in the pro ranks. As mentioned previously, Ball State moved into an impressive new stadium and improved its athletic facilities to keep pace with similar expansions of athletic programs by its rivals.

Finally, the 1950s and 1960s were a time when Ball State expanded its football program to the point where it could eventually play on a larger stage than the somewhat restrictive ICC. The Cardinal teams of the 1950s and 1960s proved that Ball State was able to play a competitive brand of football with other schools of its size in the Midwest.

At work in his office, head Coach Jim Freeman arranged his depth chart. Freeman was named ICC Coach of the Year in 1959 after his Cardinals posted a 6–2 record and were conference co-champions.

Ball State's football staff in 1959 from left to right are as follows: Sayers "Bud" Miller, the athletic trainer; and coaches Ray Louthen, Fred Kehoe, Clair Jennett, Jim Freeman, and George Mihal. Mihal was Ball State's head wrestling coach later in his career. Bud Miller was Ball State's athletic trainer from 1958–1969 and one of the leading collegiate trainers in America. He was inducted into the Ball State University Athletic Hall of Fame, posthumously, in 2000.

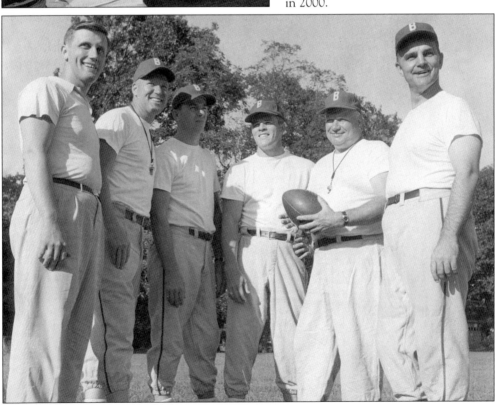

Along the sideline, Coach Freeman shouts encouragement to his players. By this time, crowds for Ball State's home football games had grown substantially. The Ball State-Butler contest in 1957 was the first contest to draw over 10,000 spectators.

A scene from football practice during the Freeman era: quarterback Ed Carozzi hands off to running back Norm Davis. An accurate passer, Corazzi was Ball State's starting quarterback in 1957, 1958, and 1959.

Three Cardinal standouts from the late 1950s: Barney Halaschak, Bob Million, and Joe Cerqueira. In 1959, Million was named the first recipient of the John Magnabosco award as the Cardinals' most valuable player in football. In 1960, Halaschak won the Magnabosco award.

Between 1952–1955, Governor "Sonny" Grady was a versatile player for Ball State. He played both offense and defense, led the team in rushing and scoring, and handled the placekicking. (BSUAHF-1988)

THE LOUTHEN ERA

Under Ray Louthen's direction, the Cardinals reached the apex of their success in football to that point in their history, either winning or sharing the conference championship for four straight seasons between 1964 and 1967. Louthen's football teams were known for their enthusiasm, hard-nosed play, and consistency. Louthen moved the Cardinals into the front ranks of the ICC and even into bowl contention. The Cardinals were truly championship-caliber teams during Louthen's tenure as head coach.

The Louthen Era in football at Ball State officially began in 1962. Known as a player's coach, Louthen congratulated the players after their last home game in 1967.

Louthen also coached Ball State's baseball team between 1959 and 1970. His teams compiled a 158–127–1 record over that period. Many of his players competed in both football and baseball.

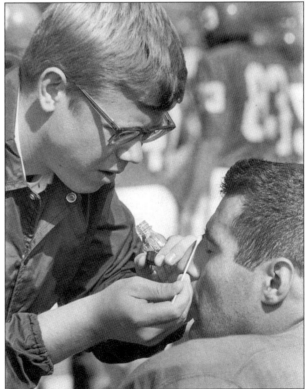

Along the sideline, a student trainer tends to a cut on the nose of lineman Elie Ghattas during a home game in 1967. Ghattas was an all-conference performer who was drafted by the New Orleans Saints in 1968.

Lineman Al Thomas comes to the bench for some medical attention. Thomas was a three-sport athlete between 1959 and 1962, competing in football, wrestling, and track and field. He was the recipient of the John Magnabosco award in 1961.(BSUAHF-1987)

While the defense is on the field, Ball State quarterback Phil Faris listens to instructions from a member of the coaching staff during a game in 1966. Faris occasionally played defense and still holds Ball State's record for the longest return of an intercepted pass, 95 yards, against Butler in 1967. Faris also won the John Magnabosco award in 1969. (BSUAHF-1990)

One of the hallmarks of the Louthen teams of the 1960s was a powerful running game. In the early 1960s, the leading ball carrier for the Cardinals was John Walker, who was also an outstanding sprinter on the track team. Walker led Ball State in rushing in 1962 with 631 yards, an average of 5.7 yards per carry. He was the recipient of the John Magnabosco award in 1962.

Ball State's leading rusher during the mid-1960s was Jim Todd, who established career rushing records in football. Todd led the Cardinals in rushing in both 1964 and 1965, averaging almost seven yards per carry. Todd was drafted by the Philadelphia Eagles in 1966. (BSUAHF-1979.)

Jim Todd breaks a tackle en route to a big gain. Todd won the John Magnabosco award in both 1964 and 1965.

Bruising fullback George Hathaway charges through a hole opened by Jim Todd (left) and the offensive line.

George Hathaway was a two-way performer for the Cardinals, playing fullback on offense and linebacker on defense. (BSUAHF-1987)

Oscar Lubke was a standout offensive lineman and all-conference player in 1966 and 1967. He was also voted to the College Division All-American team in 1967. Following his playing career at Ball State, he was drafted by the New York Jets. (BSUAHF-1995).

Amos Van Pelt, with bandage on the forehead, inherited Jim Todd's role as the Cardinals' leading ball carrier. Van Pelt led the Cardinals in rushing for three consecutive seasons, 1966, 1967, and 1968. In 1967, Van Pelt shared the John Magnabosco award with lineman Chuck Streetman.

After breaking a tackle, Amos Van Pelt strained for the goal line in Ball State's home opener in 1967. In 1969, Van Pelt was drafted by the St. Louis Cardinals of the National Football League.

Ball State's football teams of the mid-1960s featured numerous outstanding linemen. Holding the ICC championship trophy in 1967 are tackle Chuck Streetman, number 78 (BSUAHF-1993), and guard Ray McDonald, number 67 (BSUAHF-1986). Looking on at the right is end Mark Surface, number 86. Following their graduations, Streetman played briefly in the NFL; McDonald entered the teaching and coaching profession and later became executive director of the Indiana Golfers Association; and Surface became the head football coach at Marion High School. In 1988, he was named high school Coach of the Year by the Ball State University Alumni Association.

TWO SPORT STANDOUTS

Before the demands of intercollegiate sports forced specialization on college athletes, many student-athletes participated in more than one sport. Several Cardinal athletes were successful in football and other sports, such as baseball or track and field.

Tim Brown was the Cardinals' leading ball carrier between 1957 and 1958. In 1957, he averaged an astonishing 10 yards per carry. He also played on the Ball State basketball team. Brown played for the Philadelphia Eagles for six seasons before going to the Baltimore Colts, where he played for another two seasons. (BSUAHF-1976)

Better known for his outstanding career in professional baseball, especially with the Baltimore Orioles, Merv Rettenmund was also a fine football player at Ball State between 1962 and 1964 when he excelled as a ball carrier and receiver. He still holds the Ball State record for best career rushing average, 7.6 yards per carry. So outstanding was Rettenmund in football that he was drafted by the Dallas Cowboys in 1965. (BSUAHF-1976)

Frank Houk quarterbacked the 1965 Ball State team to a 9–0–1 record. He was named the MVP of the Grantland Rice Bowl in 1965. Houk also played shortstop on the baseball team. In 1966, Houk received the John Magnabosco award and later enjoyed a successful high school coaching career. (BSUAHF-1985)

Ted Huber played for the Cardinals between 1961 and 1964. He also played catcher and the outfield on the baseball team. In 1963, Huber received the John Magnabosco award. Following his graduation from Ball State, Huber became a successful high school football coach. In 1970, Huber was chosen as high school Coach of the Year by the Ball State University Alumni Association. (BSUAHF-1993)

In 1995, Huber returned to Ball State as an assistant football coach on the staff of head coach Bill Lynch. He is currently the team's assistant head coach.

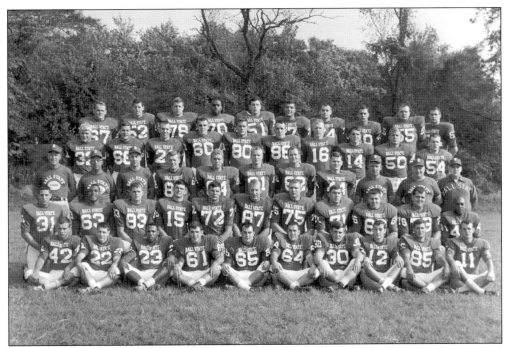

Ball State's 1965 football team, champions of the Indiana Collegiate Conference and participants in the Grantland Rice Bowl. The Cardinals tied Tennessee State, 14-14, in the bowl game on December 11, 1965.

Ball State's 1967 football team, champions of the Indiana Collegiate Conference, participants in the Grantland Rice Bowl. The Cardinals lost to Eastern Kentucky, 27-13, in the bowl game on December 9, 1967.

TRANSITION

The 1967 football season marked the end of an era and the beginning of a new period in Ball State's football history. On October 22, 1967, the Cardinals played their first game in Ball State Stadium, ending over 40 years of competition on the site of the Ball Athletic Field on University Avenue. The 1967 season was also Ray Louthen's final year as head football coach, and he yielded the reins of the team to Wave Myers, one of his assistants, for the 1968 season.

Six leaders of the 1967 team pose for a picture in Ball State's new stadium. Pictured from left to right are as follows: (front row) Oscar Lubke, Elie Ghattas, and Chuck Streetman; (back row) Ray McDonald, Amos Van Pelt, and George Hathaway.

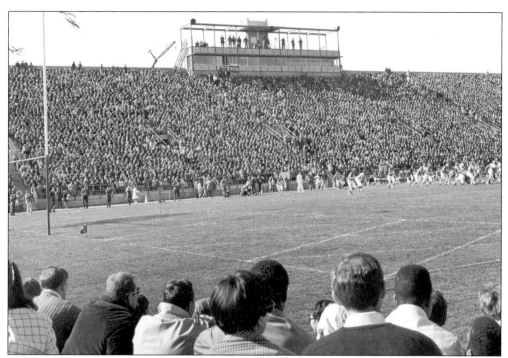

The inaugural football game played in Ball State Stadium was played on October 21, 1967. Ball State overwhelmed Butler University, 65-7.

One popular highlight of the football season, especially in the new stadium, was High School Band Day where numerous high school bands performed before the crowd.

Ball State quarterback Willard Rice was one of the standouts on the Cardinal teams of the late 1960s. Rice led the team in passing in both 1968 and 1969. Like many former Ball State players, Rice became a successful high school football coach after he graduated from Ball State.

Ray Louthen was carried from the stadium by his players after his final game as football coach in 1967. Ball State defeated Southern Illinois University, 24-6, in that game played on November 11, 1967.

Four

THE 1970S

BALL STATE JOINS THE
MID-AMERICAN CONFERENCE

In terms of Ball State University's football history, the 1970s were the most pivotal decade. In 1973, Ball State entered the Mid-American Conference (MAC), thereby becoming a competitive member of one of the most respected athletic and academic conferences in the Midwest. Once Ball State reached university status in 1965, its academic and athletic leadership set a goal of joining the MAC and being the first Indiana school to belong to the conference. The goal was achieved on May 22, 1973, when the presidents of the member institutions officially admitted Ball State to the MAC. Some skepticism existed at the time as to whether Ball State could be competitive with the other MAC universities by 1975 when it was scheduled to enter regular season play in football. However, John J Pruis, then president of Ball State, assured his fellow presidents that the Cardinals would be competitive, both "on the field and on the court," within five years of their entry into the conference. The football team's record in MAC competition between 1975 and 1980 left little doubt about Ball State's ability to accept the challenge of competing successfully in the conference.

The 1970s was also the decade, in many respects, of Coach Dave McClain. A graduate of Bowling Green, McClain had served as an assistant coach on the football staffs of Bo Schembechler at Miami University and Woody Hayes at Ohio State University before taking the head coaching position at Ball State in 1971. In Ball State's first year of MAC competition, 1975, McClain's team finished third in the conference while posting an overall record of 9–2. In 1976, Ball State won its first MAC championship in football and finished 8–3 for the season. In 1977, Ball State again finished third in the conference, despite losing just one conference game. McClain's Cardinals won their last eight games of the season and finished 9–2 once again. After the 1977 season McClain left Ball State to become the head coach at the University of Wisconsin.

The 1970s was also the decade when the Ball State football program produced many successful players who entered the professional ranks after completing their college careers. Many of these players were outstanding defensive players, such as defensive backs Terry Schmidt and Shafer Suggs, and defensive linemen Art Stringer, Ken Kremer, and Rush Brown. By the end of the decade, the professional world had clearly begun to take note of the Cardinals.

In 1978, the Cardinals won another MAC championship, this time under the direction of head coach Dwight Wallace, previously an assistant coach at the University of Colorado and a member of McClain's staff in the early 1970s. The 1978 team was perhaps Ball State's best-ever football squad, posting an 8–0 record in the conference and an overall mark of 10–1.

The Cardinals played an exciting style of football in the 1970s. Both McClain and Wallace added a strong passing game to complement the traditional emphasis on a rushing attack. The Cardinals also fielded stout defensive teams during the 1970s, especially the 1976 and 1978 units which ranked near the top, nationally, in overall scoring defense. The 1970s represented an unforgettable era in the history of Ball State football.

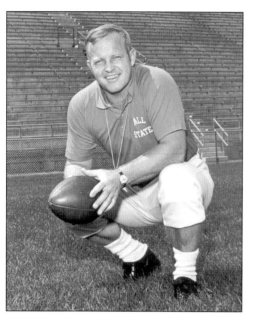

Dave McClain became the head football coach in 1971. He had a major assignment: to build the Ball State football program to the point where it could eventually compete in the Mid-American Conference. He succeeded magnificently, producing a conference champion in 1976 and two respected teams in 1975 and 1977. After the championship season of 1976, McClain was voted MAC Coach of the Year.

John J Pruis, president of Ball State University from 1968 to 1978, was instrumental in the effort to admit the university to the MAC. Pruis was a vice president at Western Michigan University, a charter member of the MAC, before accepting the presidency of Ball State. He realized the importance, both athletically and academically, of Ball State's membership in the MAC. Pruis was inducted into the Ball State University Athletic Hall of Fame in 1989.

The perspective of the new press box in Ball State Stadium presented a tremendous vantage point from which to watch the action on the field.

STANDOUTS OF THE McCLAIN ERA

Under Dave McClain's leadership, the football program produced a host of outstanding players. Many of these players distinguished themselves on defense and went on to successful careers in the NFL after completing their college careers.

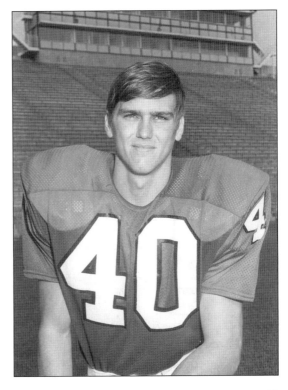

Terry Schmidt played in Ball State's defensive backfield between 1972 and 1974. He received All-American honors on the Kodak team in 1973, and played in the Coaches All-American game and the East-West Shrine game in 1974. He also won the John Magnabosco award in 1973. After his career at Ball State, Schmidt played with the New Orleans Saints in 1974 and 1975, and with the Chicago Bears Bears from 1976 to 1984. An outstanding student at Ball State, Schmidt was an Academic All-American in 1974 and the valedictorian of his class at the Loyola University Dental School in 1989. (BSUAHF-1984)

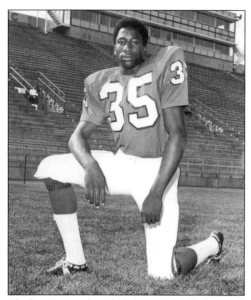

Shafer Suggs played defensive back for Ball State between 1973 and 1975. An exceptional all-around athlete, Suggs also competed in basketball for the Cardinals. In 1975, Suggs was chosen as the MAC Defensive Player of the Year, was chosen as an Associated Press second team All-American, played in the Senior Bowl, the East-West Shrine Game, and the College All-Star Game. He shared the John Magnabosco award with teammate Tim Irelan.

Art Stringer played on the defensive line and as linebacker for the Cardinals between 1971 and 1975. An all-conference player in 1975, Stringer was a member of the Houston Oilers in the NFL between 1977 and 1981. (BSUAHF-1986)

Shafer Suggs breaks up a pass intended for an opposing receiver, a familiar site at Ball State games. Suggs shares Ball State's record for career interceptions, 14, with Mike Lecklider. In 1974, Suggs tied a season record with eight interceptions, a record which he shares with Nickey Baker, who intercepted eight passes in 1965. (Muncie Newspapers-John Crozier)

Shafer Suggs occasionally returned kickoffs for the Cardinals. In 1976, he was selected in the second round of the NFL draft by the New York Jets and played for the Jets between 1976 and 1980. He also played for the Cincinnati Bengals in 1980. (BSUAHF-1987)

Maurice Harvey, seen pursuing a fumble in this photo, was a mainstay of the Cardinal secondary between 1973 and 1977. An all-conference player in both 1976 and 1977, Harvey played on Ball State's championship team in 1976. He played in the East-West Shrine Game in 1977, and was drafted by the Denver Broncos in 1978. Harvey played in the NFL between 1978 and 1984, playing for the Broncos, the Green Bay Packers, the Detroit Lions, and the Tampa Bay Buccaneers over that period. (BSUAHF-1988)(Muncie Newspapers-Brian Green)

CONTENDING FOR THE MAC CHAMPIONSHIP

Between 1975 and 1978, the Ball State Cardinals won two MAC championships and contended for the top spot on two other occasions. These strong showings surprised many football observers who did not expect the Cardinals to challenge for conference leadership so quickly. Several Cardinal players played instrumental roles in elevating Ball State to football prominence during the mid-1970s.

Art Yaroch quarterbacked the Cardinals between 1973 and 1976. He was the field general for the 1976 MAC championship team. The Cardinals opened the conference season on September 18, 1976, with a 23-6 victory over Miami University in Oxford, Ohio, a victory which set the stage for the entire season. Yaroch expertly directed the team in that victory, arguably the biggest win in Ball State's football history to that point. Yaroch led the Cardinals in passing in both 1975 and 1976. (BSUAHF-1988)

In addition to his passing skills, Art Yaroch skillfully directed Ball State's option attack, as shown in this photo. An all-conference quarterback in 1976, Yaroch won the John Magnabosco award that year. He also received an NCAA post-graduate scholarship in 1977. (Muncie Newspapers-Jerry Burney)

The 1976 Ball State University Cardinals, champions of the Mid-American Conference.

Dwight Wallace succeeded Dave McClain as Ball State's head football coach in 1978. Shown talking to players along the sideline during Ball State's victory over the University of Toledo in 1978, Wallace coached the Cardinals to their second MAC championship in football. Wallace was voted MAC Coach of the Year in 1978.

Ball State opened the 1978 season at home against Miami University. It was a must-win game for both teams, and the expressions on the faces of both Coach Wallace and the players revealed the intensity of the contest. Ball State won, 38-14.

Cardinal defensive backs Al Rzepka, number 11, and Bill Stahl, number 14, close on a Miami receiver. Stahl received all-conference honors in 1978. (Muncie Newspapers-Gary Burney.)

A familiar site from the mid-1970s: Cardinal defensive linemen Rush Brown, number 70, and Ken Kremer, number 91, pursue an opposing ball carrier. Brown and Kremer both ended their careers tied for the number of tackles for loss, 51.

Ken Kremer was a standout defensive tackle for Ball State between 1975 and 1978. He played on two championship teams, was voted to the all-conference team twice, was voted as the MAC's Outstanding Defensive Player in 1978, and was voted to the Associated Press's third team, All-America, in 1978. Finally, he won the John Magnabosco award in 1978. Following his playing career at Ball State, Kremer was a defensive lineman for the Kansas City Chiefs in the NFL between 1979 and 1984. (BSUAHF-1989)

Rush Brown played defensive tackle for Ball State between 1976 and 1979. He played on two MAC champion teams and was voted to the all-conference team in 1978 and 1979. After his playing career at Ball State, Brown was a member of the St. Louis Cardinals in the NFL between 1981 and 1983. (BSUAHF-1990)

Pictured are the Ball State Cardinals, MAC Champions, 1978.

Jim Neddeff was a dependable, consistent placekicker for Ball State during the mid-1970s. He earned all-conference honors in 1975, and played on the 1976 championship team. Neddeff holds Ball State's career record for most consecutive extra points, 36.

STRENGTH UP FRONT

During the 1970s, Ball State produced a number of stellar offensive linemen who opened holes for the running backs and protected the quarterbacks on passing plays. Several of these linemen earned recognition from the conference and from national organizations.

Doug Bell played center for Ball State in the early 1970s. He was voted as a first team All-American by the American Football Coaches Association in 1972. Bell shared the John Magnabosco award that year with quarterback Phil Donahue.

Jim Micklos played tight end for Ball State in the early 1970s. He was drafted by the New York Giants in 1975, and played offensive tackle as a professional.

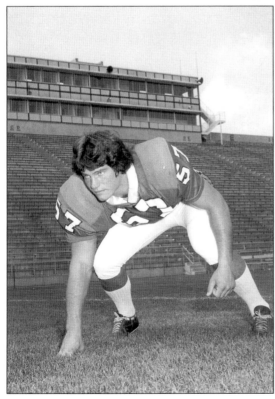

Mitch Hoban anchored Ball State's offensive line on Dave McClain's teams of the mid-1970s. In 1975 and 1976, he was voted all-conference, and in 1976, was chosen as a third team All-American by the Associated Press.

Offensive tackle Tom Broderick,
number 75, charges out to lead a
running play in 1976. A versatile player,
Broderick played center, tight end, and
tackle during his career at Ball State.

Rugged center Dave St. Clair shows the
perspiration and fatigue of a game in
1979.

QUARTERBACKING THE CARDINALS

Both Dave McClain and Dwight Wallace introduced a multiple offense during the 1970s, and the play of the quarterback became even more essential to the outcome of a football game. As the passing game grew in importance, Ball State recruited talented passers and skilled receivers to complement a solid ground game.

Phil Donahue, shown here eluding a Central Michigan tackler, quarterbacked the Cardinals from 1970 to 1972. A skilled passer, he led the Cardinals in passing each of the three years and threw 23 touchdown passes during his career. He shared the John Magnabosco award with center Doug Bell in 1972. (Muncie Newspaper-Jerry Joschko.)

Dave Wilson, number 15, shown passing against Toledo, quarterbacked the Cardinals in 1977, part of 1978, and 1979. He led the team in passing each year, and received the John Magnabosco award in 1977 and 1979. After graduating from Ball State, Wilson received a degree in theology and began a career as a chaplain to the Detroit Lions and a spiritual adviser to numerous NFL players. (BSUAHF-1990)

Mark O'Connell, shown here conferring with Coach Dwight Wallace, quarterbacked the Cardinals for part of the 1978 and 1979 campaigns, and the 1980 season. O'Connell was an all-conference selection at quarterback in 1980 and was the MAC Offensive Player of the Year.

Mark O'Connell also handled the punting duties for the Cardinals. He won the John Magnabosco award in 1980, and was voted all-conference as a punter in 1976. He was selected by the Cincinnati Bengals in the NFL draft in 1981. (BSUAHF-1991)

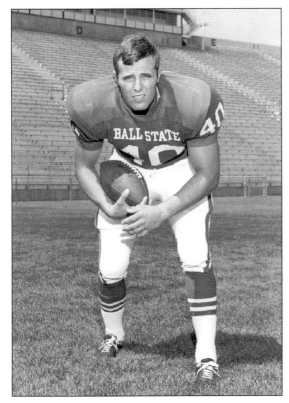

Don Burchfield played tight end for Ball State between 1968 and 1971. He was drafted by the New Orleans Saints in 1971, and also played briefly for the Chicago Fire of the World Football League (WFL) in the mid-1970s.

Rick Morrison, number 25, was Ball State's breakaway receiver in the mid-1970s. Morrison led the Cardinals, and the Mid-American Conference, in receiving in 1976 and 1977, setting a team record with 59 receptions in 1977. He was voted all-conference both years. During his career, he set Ball State records for most touchdown passes caught and most career yardage. He also holds Ball State's career record for most punt return yards, 613. (BSUAHF-1995)

Wingback Tim Clary, shown here avoiding a Central Michigan defender, was a dependable, steady receiver for the Cardinals between 1978 and 1980. Clary led Ball State in receiving in both 1978 and 1979. He especially distinguished himself in the classroom and was an Academic All-American for 1978, 1979, and 1980. (BSUAHF-1992) (Muncie Newspaper-John Crozier)

End Ray Hinton, shown here catching a pass near the goal line, was a durable lineman as well as a receiver. Hinton scored the winning touchdown in Ball State's championship-clinching victory over Western Michigan on November 11, 1978. He was voted to the all-conference team in both 1978 and 1980.

Stevie Nelson led Ball State in receiving for three consecutive seasons, 1980, 1981, and 1982. He was also an expert kickoff returner, and holds the Ball State record for the longest return, 100 yards, against Ohio University in 1980. Nelson was an all-conference selection in 1980 and 1981. (BSUAHF-1995)

CARRYING THE LOAD

Despite the success of the Ball State passing game during the 1970s, the Cardinals still possessed a strong ground game. Several running backs produced outstanding seasons during this decade and joined the ranks of such runners as Jim Todd and Amos Van Pelt as the Cardinals' primary ball carriers.

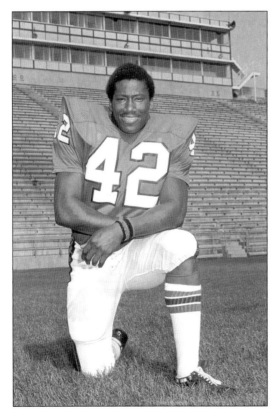

Dave Blake was Ball State's leading ball carrier in 1974. He was the first Cardinal to rush for more than 1,000 yards in a single season when he gained 1,125 yards. Blake also had six consecutive games when he rushed for more than 100 yards, a Ball State record. He received the John Magnabosco award in 1974.

Dependable Earl Taylor was Ball State's primary ball carrier in 1975 and 1976. He carried for 1,017 yards in 1976, and set a Ball State record for most yards gained in a single game when he rushed for 260 yards against Eastern Michigan.

Mark Bornholdt, shown scoring against Bowling Green, holds the single season record for most touchdowns when he scored 19 touchdowns in 1979. Known as "Mr. Six," Bornholdt ranks second, all-time, to Michael Blair, among Ball State running backs for touchdowns scored with a total of 30. Bornholdt was also one of the top scorers in the country in 1979, with 114 points.

DEFENSE WINS CHAMPIONSHIPS

One often quoted football proverb holds that "offense wins games but defense wins championships." Ball State's football teams of the 1970s, especially the championship teams of 1976 and 1978, were known for their stellar defensive units. The 1976 team held the opposition to 10 or fewer points in 8 of its 11 games. The 1978 team never yielded more than 17 points in any game, recorded 4 shutouts, and held the opposition to 7 points or less in 7 of its 11 games. In addition to a strong defensive line, the Cardinals had an outstanding linebacking corps and a hard-hitting secondary.

Mike Lecklider played safety for the Cardinals between 1974 and 1976. Coach Dave McClain referred to Lecklider as the "steadying influence in the secondary." A member of the 1976 championship team, Lecklider shares Ball State's career record for interceptions, 14, with Shafer Suggs.

Jeff Hilles played in the defensive secondary between 1976 and 1978. The son of Jim Hilles, Ball State's defensive coordinator during the McClain era, Hilles played on the 1976 and 1978 championship teams. When Dave McClain left Ball State in 1977, Jim Hilles joined his staff at the University of Wisconsin. Following McClain's death, Hilles was the head coach at Wisconsin during the 1986 season.

Jon Hoke played in the defensive secondary for four seasons between 1976 and 1979. After his career at Ball State, Hoke played in the National Football League with the Chicago Bears.

Jon Hoke confers with a defensive coach during a time-out. After his playing career in college and the NFL, Hoke pursued the coaching profession in the collegiate ranks. He is currently an assistant coach and defensive coordinator at the University of Florida.

Cardinal defensive backs Al Rzepka, number 11, and Jeff Hilles, number 40, close in for a tackle during the Miami game in 1978. Rzepka returned to Ball State as an assistant football coach in the mid-1980s.(Muncie Newspapers-Garry Burney)

Dennis Gunden, number 95, was a durable linebacker between 1976 and 1980. He was a standout performer on the 1978 championship team.

Cardinal safety Sel Drain confers with his defensive coaches while the offense is on the field. Drain moved into the starting lineup in 1979, his freshman year, and was a mainstay of the defensive unit for the rest of his career. An all-conference performer in 1982, Drain later played professional for Toronto in the Canadian Football League.

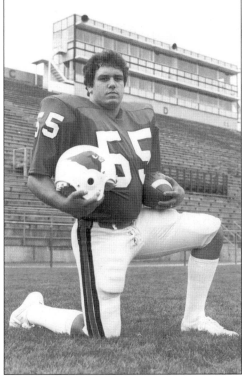

Brady Hoke teamed with Dennis Gunden and Kelly George at linebacker for part of his career at Ball State. He was also a teammate of his brother, Jon Hoke, on the 1977, 1978, and 1979 teams. Brady Hoke is currently an assistant coach at the University of Michigan.

Kelly George moves in for a tackle on an Eastern Michigan ball carrier. An all-conference performer in 1982, George also won the John Magnabosco award that year. (BSUAHF-1994) (Muncie Newspapers-Loren Fisher)

Kelly George was a member of Ball State's linebacking corps between 1979 and 1982. He joins the defensive unit for a brief respite before going back into action.

A familiar scene from the 1978 season: brothers Jon Hoke, number 37, and Brady Hoke, 55, move in for a tackle.

Five

THE 1980S

DECLINE AND RESURGENCE

Following Ball State's MAC championship season in 1978, the football program experienced mostly mediocre seasons through much of the next decade. Winning seasons matched losing seasons for most of this period, and the Cardinals slipped from being conference contenders to occupying a spot in the middle of the league.

In 1985, Paul Schudel replaced Dwight Wallace as Ball State's head football coach and the football program began another era. Schudel graduated from Miami University of Ohio, and was an assistant coach at the University of Michigan under head coach Bo Schembechler before taking the head coaching assignment at Ball State. Schudel's tenure lasted from 1985–1994, with the Cardinals posting a 60–48–4 record over that period. Schudel became Ball State's second winningest coach, ranking behind John Magnabosco. Under Schudel's direction, the football program began a resurgence in the late 1980s, and the Cardinals returned to the front ranks of the conference. Ball State won a league championship in 1989, and another in 1993. Winning the MAC championship brought a new reward, participation in a post-season bowl game. The Cardinals played in the California Raisin Bowl in 1989, losing to Fresno State 27-6, and in the Las Vegas Bowl in 1993, losing to Utah State, 42-33.

Like previous eras in Ball State's football history, the 1980s witnessed its share of excitement. The Cardinals emphasized the passing game throughout much of the 1980s and Ball State fans were treated to emergence of several new offensive standouts. The world of college football also began to change as the sport's governing bodies, especially the NCAA, began to pay more attention to academic issues, such as the grade-point averages of scholar-athletes as well as their graduation rates. Several Ball State football players distinguished themselves in the classroom, as well as on the field, in response to this new emphasis. The NCAA also pressed the member institutions in Division I football to upgrade and modernize their athletic facilities. The 1980s signaled the beginning of another demanding era in football at Ball State, but it was clear, by the end of the decade, that the Cardinals had risen to the occasion.

Paul Schudel became Ball State's head football coach on December 11, 1984. He is shown in this picture with Don Purvis, Ball State's athletic director.

Shown along the sidelines during a game at Ball State Stadium, Schudel's teams won MAC championships in 1989 and 1993. After each season, Schudel was named conference Coach of the Year.

Ball State players rushed onto the field and doused their coaches after a hard-fought victory over Eastern Michigan during their championship season in 1989.

At the football team's awards banquet following the 1989 season, Schudel poses for a picture with Morry Mannies, a Ball State alumnus, and the "Voice of the Cardinals." Mannies has been the play-by-play announcer for radio broadcasts of Ball State's football and basketball games since 1956. He was inducted into the Ball State University Athletic Hall of Fame in 1985.

Pictured are the 1989 Ball State Cardinals, champions of the Mid-American Conference.

David Riley, Ball State's quarterback in 1988 and 1989, led the team's explosive offense. Riley led the Cardinals in passing both seasons and was an all-conference performer in 1989. He also won the John Magnabosco award in 1989.

The honors kept rolling in for David Riley in 1989. After the season, Riley received the MAC's Vern Smith Award as the conference's Most Valuable Player. He is shown in this photo with Coach Schudel. Riley was also voted as the league's Offensive Player of the Year. After finishing his playing career at Ball State, Riley played professional football briefly in Europe.

CARRYING THE LOAD

Ball State's ground game remained strong in the 1980s. Several outstanding ball carriers typified the hard-nosed rushing attack which historically was a central element in Ball State's offense.

Bernie Parmalee led Ball State in rushing in 1987, 1989, and 1990. In 1987 and 1990, he rushed for more than 1,000 yards. The MAC Freshman of the Year in 1987, Parmalee was an all-conference selection in 1988 and 1990, and received the John Magnabosco award in 1990. After his college career, Parmalee played for the Miami Dolphins and the New York Jets.

Cardinal tailback Adam Wilson prepares to stiff-arm a Northern Illinois defender in a game at Ball State Stadium in 1987. The Cardinals won the game, 42-17.

Terry Lymon was Ball State's leading ball carrier for three consecutive seasons, 1981, 1982, and 1983. Along with Terry Schmid, who led the Cardinals in rushing in 1971, 1972, and 1973, Lymon was the only Ball State running back to lead the Cardinals in rushing for three straight seasons. In this photo, Lymon is shown breaking away for a long gain in a game against the University of Toledo.

Carlton Campbell was a durable runner for Ball State in the mid-1980s. He led the Cardinals in rushing in 1985 and 1986 with 747 yards and 688 yards, respectively.

THE CARDINALS TAKE TO THE AIR

During the 1980s, Ball State developed a formidable passing attack. With several outstanding quarterbacks and a corps of fast receivers, the Cardinals routinely passed between 25 and 35 times per game. The passing game made for some exciting moments as the Cardinals set new records for passes, receptions, and touchdown passes.

Neil Britt stands in the pocket, searching for an open receiver. Britt quarterbacked the Cardinals in 1983 and 1984. In 1983, he set a school record for pass attempts, 348, completions, 206, and most yards gained passing, 2,377.

Wade Kosakowski quarterbacked the Cardinals in 1985, 1986, and 1987. An accurate passer, Kosakowski ranked near the top of the conference in passing efficiency.

Tight end Ron Duncan snares a pass and heads upfield in Ball State's game against Purdue University in 1985. Duncan was an all-conference performer in 1986 and 1987, and a three-time Academic All-American in 1985, 1986, and 1987. In 1988, he received an NCAA post-graduate scholarship to attend medical school. (BSUAHF-1998)

Tight end Eugene Riley was an imposing blocker and receiver between 1986 and 1989. He was an all-conference selection in 1988 and 1989. In 1988, he led the Cardinals in receiving with 41 pass receptions. After completing his playing career at Ball State, Riley signed free agent contracts with the Indianapolis Colts in 1990 and the Detroit Lions in 1991.

Dave Naumcheff holds the career record for most yards gained receiving in a single season, 1,065. He set that record in 1983, the first Ball State receiver to gain over 1,000 yards in a single season. Naumcheff was an all-conference selection and winner of the John Magnabosco award in 1983. (BSUAHF-1999)

Ricky George was a wide receiver for Ball State between 1983 and 1986. In this photo, he is shown hauling in a touchdown pass during a game in 1985. George was an all-conference selection in 1986 when he caught 55 passes for 569 yards. In 1986, he shared the John Magnabosco award with place kicker John Diettrich.

Deon Chester tries to elude two tacklers after catching a pass. Chester played for the Cardinals between 1984 and 1987, leading the team in receiving in 1987 with 50 catches for 838 yards. After graduating from Ball State, Chester pursued a coaching career in the collegiate ranks, including a brief time as an assistant coach at Ball State.

Ball State's offense required a strong offensive line. In this photo, center Rick Chitwood leads on a running play. Chitwood played for the Cardinals between 1980 and 1983 and was an all-conference performer in 1983. An outstanding student, Chitwood was an Academic All-American in 1982 and 1983, received an NCAA post-graduate scholarship in 1984, and was recognized as a scholar-athlete by the National Football Foundation Hall of Fame in 1984. (BSUAHF-1994)

Offensive tackle Ed Konopasek protects the pocket for quarterback Neil Britt during a game against Western Michigan in 1984. Konopasek played for the Cardinals between 1983 and 1986. In 1987, he signed a free agent contract with the Green Bay Packers.

Offensive tackle Mark Boggs blocks during a game against Central Michigan in 1985. Boggs played professionally with the Indianapolis Colts in 1987.

Center Ted Ashburn anchored the Ball State line between 1986 and 1989. In 1989, he was honored as an Academic All-American, as a scholar-athlete by the National Football Foundation and Hall of Fame, and received an NCAA post-graduate scholarship.

THE KICKING GAME

During the 1980s, the value of the kicking game took on an added importance for the Cardinals as two of its place kickers, John Diettrich and Kenny Stucker, became major offensive weapons for the team. Prior to the arrival of Diettrich and Stucker, Ball State's kicking game had been solid and dependable, but not the potent offensive weapon which it became in the 1980s.

John Diettrich virtually re-wrote the Ball State record book for placekickers during his career between 1983 and 1986. He holds the record for most field goals in a career, 63; most field goals in a season, 25, in 1985; and most field goals in a single game, 5, against Eastern Michigan in 1985. He also holds the career record for the longest field goal, 62 yards, against Ohio University in 1986. Diettrich was an all-conference performer in 1985 and 1986 and shared the John Magnabosco award with receiver Ricky George in 1986. Named to several All-American teams, Diettrich played in the East-West Shrine game in 1986. After leaving Ball State, he signed a free agent contract with the Houston Oilers in 1987. (BSUAHF-1997)

Kenny Stucker succeeded John Diettrich as Ball State's place kicker during the late 1980s. Stucker played for Ball State between 1988 and 1991, and ranks second to Diettrich in the number of field goals in a career, 92, and second to Brent Lockliear, in number of extra points, 93. Following his senior year, Stucker played in the Blue-Gray all-star game. He has also pursued a career in the Arena Football League and has been one of its all-time leading placekickers.

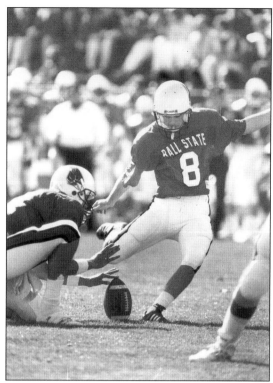

In addition to his place kicking duties, Kenny Stucker occasionally handled the punting for the Cardinals.

DEFENSIVE STANDOUTS

Ball State's defense units produced a number of outstanding players during the 1980s. In particular, Ball State's linebacking corps—led by such hard-hitters as Brad Saar, Greg Garnica, and Tim Walton—were especially strong.

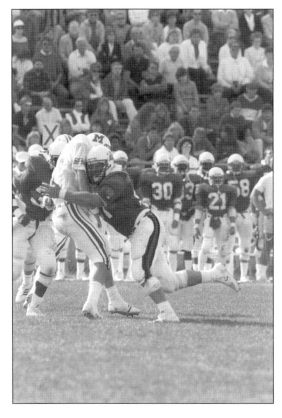

Defensive tackle Troy Schultz moves in for a sack of the quarterback in Ball State's game against Miami University in 1985. Schultz was an all-conference selection in 1986.

Jerome Davis played the nose guard position for Ball State in 1984 and 1985. In this photo, he fends off blockers in Ball State's game against Miami University in 1985. Davis played for Ball State after transferring from Illinois Valley Community College.

Mose Carter, Ball State's nose guard, penetrates the offensive line in Ball State's game against Indiana State in the Hoosier Dome in 1986. Carter was an all-conference performer in 1988.

Defensive tackle Ralph Wize sheds a block from one of Western Michigan's offensive linemen in action at Ball State Stadium in 1988. Wize was an all-conference selection in 1989, Ball State's championship season.

Nose guard Craig Newburg rushes the passer in action at Ball State Stadium in 1980. Newburg was an all-conference selection in 1981 and also won the John Magnabosco award that season.

Ball State linebacker Brad Saar moves in for a tackle in a game against Miami University in 1985. A transfer from Penn State, Saar was the leading tackler for the Cardinal defense in 1985. Saar set a Ball State season record in 1985 with 169 tackles and also won the John Magnabosco award.

Greg Garnica, number 54, and Tim Walton, number 57, were a potent linebacking duo in the late 1980s for Ball State. Walton was an all-conference selection and winner of the John Magnabosco award in 1988. He later played in the NFL and in the World League of American Football.

Greg Garnica responds enthusiastically to a fumble recovery. Garnica was the MAC Defensive Player of the Year in 1987, 1988, and 1989, the only athlete to win the award for three consecutive years. He holds Ball State's career records for most tackles, 689, and is tied for first, with defensive lineman Henry Hall, in most fumble recoveries, 6. He is also tied for second, with defensive back Terry Schmidt, for most career interceptions, 13.

Ball State cornerback Leo Porter prepares to cover an Indiana State receiver. Porter played in the Ball State secondary between 1988 and 1991.

Ball State safety David Haugh shadows a receiver from Ohio University in 1987. Haugh was an all-conference selection and an Academic All-American in 1989.

Ball State safety Troy Hoffer positions himself for the start of a play in 1990 at Ball State Stadium. Hoffer was an Academic All-American in 1991 and 1992, and he won an NCAA post-graduate scholarship in 1992.

Six

THE 1990S AND BEYOND

A TIME OF

CONTINUOUS CHALLENGE

During the 1990s, Ball State University's football program experienced a unique set of highs and lows. The Cardinals won their third MAC championship in football in 1993, and earned a trip to the Las Vegas Bowl. The championship in 1993 was followed by another league title in 1996, and a second visit to the Las Vegas Bowl. Facing ever-stiffer competition, however, the Cardinals encountered some losing seasons later in the decade. Then, in the 2000 campaign, the Cardinals finished strongly, causing Ball State's football supporters to look optimistically toward the 2001 season.

Ball State's football program continued to produce a number of outstanding players who successfully entered the professional ranks after finishing their collegiate playing careers. Players such as Keith McKenzie, Cory Gilliard, Brad Maynard, and Blaine Bishop were four Cardinals who became recognized performers in the National Football League. In fact, McKenzie, Maynard, and Bishop all played in Super Bowls, and Bishop was an NFL Pro Bowl performer.

The football program also experienced a change in leadership during the mid-1990s. Paul Schudel left Ball State in 1995 to accept an assistant coaching position with the University of Illinois. Bill Lynch, formerly an assistant coach at both Ball State and Indiana University, became the Cardinals' 12th head football coach after Schudel's departure. Lynch inherited a program with the toughest playing schedule in the school's history. In addition to the demanding MAC schedule, Ball State played such nationally-ranked programs as the University of Florida, Auburn University, the University of Kansas, Iowa State University, and Big Ten opponents such as the University of Wisconsin, the University of Minnesota, Indiana University, and Purdue University. To meet the challenge of a more rigorous NCAA Division 1 schedule, Ball State upgraded its training and athletic facilities, building a new lighted practice field with an artificial turf playing surface in 1998, and a new training building, scheduled for completion in the fall 2001. The seating capacity of Ball State Stadium was also increased substantially, expanding to over 21,000 by 1996.

The Cardinals changed the design of their helmet in 1990, replacing the design which they had used since 1971. The previous design, of course, resembled the helmet style of the St. Louis Cardinals (now the Arizona Cardinals) of the National Football League.

Mike Neu, Ball State's quarterback from 1990 to 1993, celebrates the Cardinals' come-from-behind victory against the University of Toledo in the Homecoming game, October 9, 1993. Ball State defeated Toledo, 31-30, rallying from a 30-3 deficit with just 4:10 remaining in the third quarter. Neu's touchdown pass to receiver Erin McCray as time expired tied the score, 30-30. After McCray's touchdown, Matt Swart kicked his fourth extra point of the game to win it for the Cardinals, 31-30.

Ball State players celebrate on the sideline after winning the MAC championship in 1993. Leading the cheers are offensive linemen Andy Berry, number 77, and Jose Munoz, number 71.

Paul Schudel displays the MAC Championship trophy, surrounded by Mike Neu, number 14, and safety Darrell Graham, number 13.

Don Purvis, Ball State's athletics director in 1993, extends post-game congratulations to Coach Schudel, Jose Munoz, and running back Tony Nibbs, number 33.

Mike Neu quarterbacked the Cardinals for four consecutive seasons, 1990–1993, and holds Ball State's records for most yards passing in a single game, 469; most yards passing in a career, 6,221; most passes attempted, 970; most completions, 580; and most touchdown passes for a career, 43. He compiled a .657 completion percentage in 1993, and won the Vern Smith Award as the conference's Most Valuable Player, as well as the conference Offensive Player of the Year award. After finishing his career at Ball State, Neu played in the Canadian Football League and the Arena Football League. Finally, Neu was an all-conference selection and winner of the John Magnabosco award in 1993. He has also coached in the Arena Football League.

Blaine Bishop was a standout performer in the Ball State secondary between 1989 and 1992. He played in both the Senior Bowl and the Blue-Gray all-star game in 1992. After finishing his career at Ball State, Bishop was drafted by the Houston Oilers in 1993. Since then, he has enjoyed an outstanding professional career with the Oilers and with the Tennessee Titans. Bishop has been a Pro Bowl selection and played in the 2000 Super Bowl between the Titans and the St. Louis Rams.

Blaine Bishop combines with fellow Cardinal defenders Carl Kendrick, number 92, and Mark Parris, number 58, to stop a Miami runner in 1992. Kendrick and Parris both played for the Cardinals between 1989 and 1992.

Michael Blair was a hard-nosed runner who led the Cardinals in rushing in 1995 and 1996. He ranks third on Ball State's record for rushing yards in a career with 3,051 yards, and he holds the record for most touchdowns in a career, 31. He was the MAC Freshman of the Year and an all-conference selection in 1993. Blair has played professionally with Green Bay Packers, the Cleveland Browns and, most recently, in the XFL.

Pictured are the 1993 Ball State Cardinals, champions of the Mid-American Conference

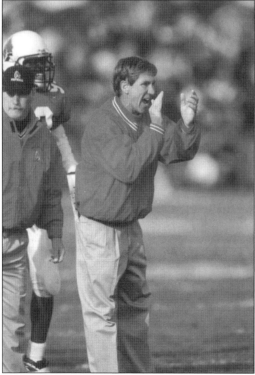

An energetic coach, Bill Lynch shouts encouragement to the players from the sidelines.

THE LYNCH ERA BEGINS

Paul Schudel's departure in 1995 led to the hiring of Bill Lynch as the Cardinals' head football coach. An outstanding collegiate athlete in both football and basketball at Butler University, Lynch was the head football coach at Butler before joining Schudel's staff between 1990 and 1992. He spent the 1993 and 1994 seasons at Indiana University as the quarterback's coach. He returned to Ball State as head football coach in 1995.

In Bill Lynch's second season as head coach, the Cardinals won their fourth conference championship.

Ball State produced some national caliber defensive players during the Lynch era. These included safety Cory Gilliard, an all-conference selection in both 1995 and 1996. Gilliard also played in the East-West Shrine Game and has played for the Denver Broncos, the New Orleans Saints, and the New England Patriots.

Keith McKenzie was a hard-hitting defensive end and linebacker for the Cardinals between 1992 and 1995. He was an all-conference selection and recipient of the John Magnabosco award in 1995. When he entered the professional ranks in 1996, he played for the Green Bay Packers and made the first tackle of Super XXI in 1997.

Brad Maynard booms a punt from deep in Ball State territory. One of the greatest players in Ball State's football history, Maynard punted for the Cardinals between 1993 and 1996. He holds Ball State's records for best single-season punting average, 46.5 yards in 1995; best career punting average, 44.2 yards; most punts, 242; and most punting yards, 10,702. He was a three-time all-conference selection, a consensus All-American in 1995 and 1996, the Vern Smith Award winner as the MAC Most Valuable Player in 1996, and the MAC Defensive Player of the Year in 1996. He shared the John Magnabosco award in 1996 with linebacker Aaron Gralak.

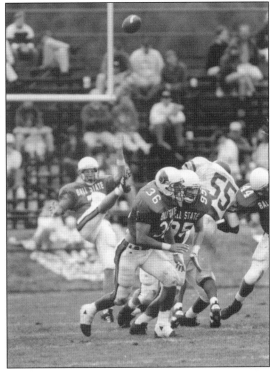

Brad Maynard and Bill Lynch get re-acquainted at a Ball State football outing. Maynard played in the Senior Bowl in 1996, and was drafted by the New York Giants in 1997. He played in the 2001 Super Bowl.

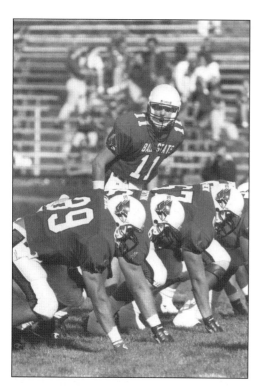

Brent Baldwin replaced Mike Neu as the Ball State quarterback in 1994. Baldwin quarterbacked the Cardinals in 1994, 1995, and 1996, leading the team in passing each year. He directed the team to a MAC championship in 1996, and holds Ball State's record for best completion percentage in a career, .657 (392 of 597). Baldwin has pursued a collegiate coaching career and currently is an assistant coach at Ball State.

Coach Lynch poses with former Cardinals currently playing in the professional ranks. From left to right are as follows: Michael Blair, Brad Maynard, Cory Gilliard, Keith McKenzie, and Bill Lynch.

Here are the 1996 Ball State Cardinals, champions of the Mid-American Conference.

FIREPOWER ON OFFENSE

Ball State's offensive teams in the 1990s featured the customary blend of running and passing which had characterized previous teams. The Cardinals continued to field running backs who were capable of gaining more than 1,000 yards per season, as well as dependable quarterbacks and swift receivers.

Corey Croom led Ball State in rushing in 1991 and 1992 with 1,053 yards and 1,157 yards, respectively. An all-conference selection both seasons, Croom also won the John Magnabosco award in 1992. After his career at Ball State, Croom played in the NFL for the New England Patriots between 1993 and 1995. Croom holds Ball State's single season record for rushing attempts, 301.

Tony Nibbs eludes a Purdue tackler. Nibbs succeeded Corey Croom as the Cardinals' leading ball carrier in 1993 and 1994. Nibbs holds Ball State's single-season rushing record with 1,210 yards (5.5 yards per carry) in 1994. Nibbs won the John Magnabosco award, and was an all-conference selection in 1994. He played for the Cleveland Browns in 1995.

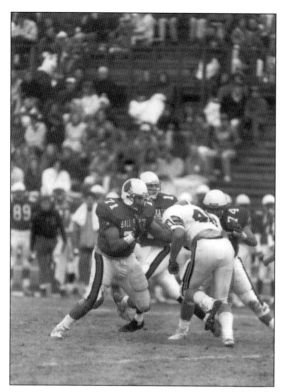

Supporting the Cardinals offensive attack between 1990 and 1993 was offensive tackle Jose Munoz, shown here in a game against Bowling Green in 1991. Munoz was an all-conference performer in 1993, and played professionally in the National Football League and the Arena Football League.

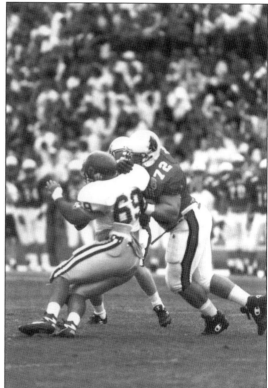

Tony Roush was a stalwart offensive tackle between 1993 and 1996. In this picture, Roush is shown delivering a crushing block on an opposing defender. Roush was an all-conference selection in 1996.

LeAndre Moore looks for a hole in Ball State's game against Purdue in 1997. Moore was Ball State's primary ball carrier in 1997 and 1998. Moore gained 909 yards in 1998, and had five games where he gained more than 100 yards. He received the John Magnabosco award in 1998.

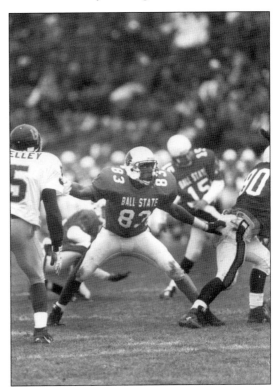

Tight end Ted Freeman was an excellent blocker and pass catcher for Ball State between 1992 and 1994. An all-conference player in 1993, Freeman is shown blocking for a field goal attempt against the University of Toledo in 1992.

Brian Oliver led the Cardinals in receiving in 1992 and 1993. An all-conference performer in 1993, he is shown here breaking free after a reception in a game against Kent State University in 1991. Oliver holds many of Ball State's career records for pass receiving, including most touchdown passes caught in a single season, 10 (1993), and in a career, 24. Oliver gained 297 yards in receiving in Ball State's comeback victory over the University of Toledo in 1993. Oliver played professionally in the Canadian Football League and the Arena Football League.

Adrian Reese, number 20, breaks free with a pass reception in Ball State's game against Miami University in 1998. Reese led the Cardinals in pass receiving in 1997, 1998, and 1999. He ranks near the top for Cardinal receivers for most pass receptions and most yardage. He was the recipient of the John Magnabosco award in 1999.

THE DEFENSE NEVER RESTS

During the 1990s, the Ball State football program produced another group of outstanding defensive performers. In addition to punter Brad Maynard and other NFL-bound defenders such as Blaine Bishop, Cory Gilliard, and Keith McKenzie, numerous other defensive players contributed to the team.

Henry Hall was a strong presence at defensive end for Ball State between 1989 and 1992. An all-conference selection in 1991 and 1992, Hall holds Ball State's career record for tackles for loss, 53, and is tied with Greg Garnica for most fumble recoveries, 6.

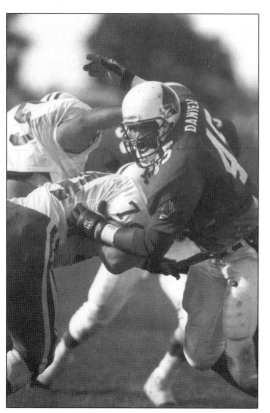

Defensive lineman Jermaine Daniels plays off an opponent's block in 1993. Following the 1995 season, Daniels was named a tri-captain of the football team. He died tragically in an auto accident in 1996.

Defensive tackle Damon Hummel prepares to penetrate Purdue's offensive line during the Purdue-Ball State game in 1995. Hummel played for the Cardinals between 1995 and 1998, and was an all-conference performer in 1996. He played professional football for the Toronto Argonauts of the Canadian Football League in 1999.

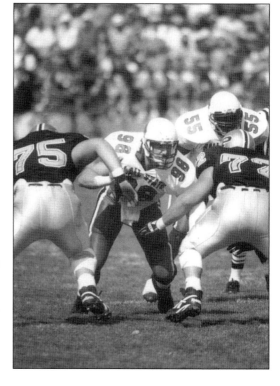

Defensive end Wilber McDonald sets up along the line of scrimmage in Ball State's game against Utah State in the Las Vegas Bowl in 1996. McDonald played for the Cardinals in 1996 and 1997, leading the team with 10 quarterback sacks in 1997.

Mark Parris plays off a block from a Western Michigan lineman in 1991. Parris played linebacker for the Cardinals between 1989 and 1992. He was an all-conference performer and winner of the John Magnabosco award in 1991.

Kevin Johnson was a stalwart linebacker for Ball State in 1993 and 1994. He holds Ball State's season record for most tackles, 204, set in 1993. Johnson's total of 196 tackles in 1994 ranks second in that category.

Ball State linebackers Keith McKenzie, number 59, and Aaron Gralak, number 36, are poised for the attack during a game in 1996. Gralak was an all-conference selection in 1996, and he shared the John Magnabosco award with punter Brad Maynard that year.

Copatric Dartis played in Ball State's defensive secondary between 1990 and 1993, and was a team captain in 1993. In this photo, Dartis returns an interception against Bowling Green in 1991. Dartis led the team with four interceptions in 1991.

Raphael Ball goes into pass coverage in action during a game in 1995. He was an all-conference selection in 1996, and played professionally in the National Football League.

Raphaol Ball anticipates the action during a game in 1994. After his career at Ball State, Raphaol Ball played for the Miami Dolphins in the NFL and the British Columbia Lions in the CFL. Raphaol Ball is the twin brother of Raphael Ball.

Injuries are an unfortunate but inescapable part of college football. In this photo, Ball State trainers Tony Cox, left, and Rex Sharp, right, tend to Ball State linebacker Jeff Phelps.

Shown kicking off against Indiana University in Bloomington, Brent Lockliear handled Ball State's placekicking duties between 1994 and 1997. Lockliear ranks first, all-time, with 103 extra points, and ranks third, behind John Diettrich and Kenny Stucker with 38 field goals. He was an all-conference selection in 1996.

Damon Keller booms a punt in Ball State's game against Bowling Green at Ball State Stadium. Keller was Ball State's punter between 1990 and 1992, and was an all-conference selection in 1991. He punted 89 times for 3,183 yards in 1992, setting single-season records in both categories.

Appendix A

Recipients of the John V. Magnabosco award as Ball State University's Most Valuable Player in Football

1959	Bob Million
1960	Barney Halaschak
1961	Al Thomas
1962	John Walker
1963	Ted Huber
1964	Jim Todd
1965	Jim Todd
1966	Frank Houk
1967	Charles Streetman and Amos Van Pelt
1968	Ed Alley
1969	Phil Faris
1970	Jerry Burns
1971	Rusty Clifford
1972	Doug Bell and Phil Donahue
1973	Terry Schmidt
1974	Dave Blake
1975	Tim Irelan and Shafer Suggs
1976	Art Yaroch
1977	Dave Wilson
1978	Ken Kremer
1979	Dave Wilson
1980	Mark O'Connell
1981	Craig Newburg
1982	Kelly George
1983	Dave Naumcheff
1984	Mike Leuck
1985	Brad Saar
1986	John Diettrich and Ricky George
1987	Deon Chester
1988	Tim Walton
1989	David Riley
1990	Bernie Parmalee
1991	Mark Parris
1992	Corey Croom
1993	Mike Neu
1994	Tony Nibbs
1995	Keith McKenzie
1996	Aaron Gralak and Brad Maynard
1997	Howard Simms
1998	LeAndre Moore
1999	Adrian Reese
2000	Talmadge Hill

Appendix B

Recipients of the High School Football Coach of the Year Award
By The Ball State University Alumni Association

1957	William McClain, '50, Noblesville
1958	Charles "Wave" Myers, '50, Huntington
1959	Victor Overman, '46, Michigan City
1960	William Lynch, '49, New Carlisle
1961	Hubert Etchison, '39, Richmond
1962	Hubert Etchison, '39, Richmond
1963	Hubert Etchison, '39, Richmond
1964	Robert Baker, '51, Madison Heights
1965	Jack Lowe, '57 North Liberty
1966	Donald Wiggs, '59, Winchester
1967	Hubert Etchison, '39, Richmond
1968	James Hollibaugh, '51, Logansport
1969	Steve Lookabaugh, '64, Delta
1970	Ted Huber, '67, Hamilton Heights
1971	William Siderewicz, '61, Martinsville
1972	William Doba, '62, Mishawaka
1973	Robert Van Camp, '50, South Bend Washington
1974	William Doba, '62, Mishawaka
1975	David Land, '69, Delta
1976	William Nixon, '62, Plymouth
1977	William Nixon, '62, Plymouth
1978	Victor Overman, '46, Brownsburg
1979	Myron Dickerson, '61, Fort Wayne Northside
1980	Larry "Bud" Wright, '63, Sheridan
1981	Leland Etzler, '62, Woodland
1982	Frank O'Shea, '63, McCutcheon
1983	Joseph Jackson, '55, Anderson Highland
1984	George Conn, '72, Concord
1985	Myron Dickerson, '61, Wawasee
1986	Michael Hawley, '68, Fort Wayne Snider
1987	Larry "Bud" Wright, '63, Sheridan
1988	Mark Surface, '68, Marion
1989	Gerald Vlasic, '62, Hammond Bishop Noll
1990	David Wilhelm, '69, Southwood
1991	John Fallis, '66, Greencastle
1992	Daniel Robinson, '73, Northwestern
1993	Ernie Beck, '59, West Lafayette
1994	Martin Huber, '77, Bremen
1995	John Hendryx, '86, Carroll
1996	John Hendryx, '86, Carroll
1997	Donald Willard, '64, Knightstown
1998	Larry "Bud" Wright, '63, Sheridan
1999	Bob Gaddis, '78, Evansville Reitz
2000	Grant Zgunda, '90, Delta